CW00665256

**Nikki van der Gaag** is a freelance writer, editor and evaluator on development issues. Prior to this she was editorial director at the Panos Institute and co-editor of the **New Internationalist** magazine.

NEW INTERNATIONALIST

**Trigger Issues**
One small item – one giant impact

Other titles:
**Mosquito**
**Kalashnikov**

**About the New Internationalist**
The **New Internationalist** is an independent not-for-profit publishing co-operative. Our mission is to report on issues of global justice. We publish informative current affairs and popular reference titles, complemented by world food, photography and gift books as well as calendars, diaries, maps and posters – all with a global justice world view.

If you like this **Trigger Issue** book you'll also love the **New Internationalist** magazine. Each month it takes a different subject such as Trade Justice, Nuclear Power or Iraq, exploring and explaining the issues in a concise way; the magazine is full of photos, charts and graphs as well as music, film and book reviews, country profiles, interviews and news.

To find out more about the **New Internationalist**, visit our website at:
**www.newint.org**

# DIAMONDS

**Nikki van der Gaag**

NEW INTERNATIONALIST

**Trigger Issues: Diamonds**
First published in the UK in 2006 by
New Internationalist™ Publications Ltd
55 Rectory Road,
Oxford OX4 1BW, UK
**www.newint.org**
New Internationalist is a registered trade mark.

Series editor: Troth Wells
Design by New Internationalist Publications Ltd.

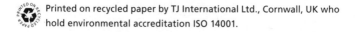 Printed on recycled paper by TJ International Ltd., Cornwall, UK who
hold environmental accreditation ISO 14001.

British Library Cataloguing-in-Publication Data.
A catalogue record for this book is available from the British Library.

Library of Congress Cataloguing-in-Publication Data.
A catalogue for this book is available from the Library of Congress.

ISBN 10: 1-904456-29-4
ISBN 13: 978-1904456-292

# Contents

# Introduction

**Diamond. The word itself seems to sparkle. Diamonds** are seduction, status and wealth. They are often the only jewels in an engagement ring. They are the hardest substance on earth. Formed many millions of years ago, their glitter is hidden in the mud until they are mined, polished, cut, set and encased in gold or silver. Just why do we value diamonds above rubies, sapphires or emeralds? They are less rare than other gems, so what makes them so special – and so expensive? And how have they come to be the symbol of love and status?

Diamonds, which today are mined in 25 different countries, were originally found in India, dripping from the fingers of 13th-century kings. From early days, the gems were used as tools as well as jewelry; for fashioning beads and engraving letters. It was believed that owning a diamond could give you health and virtue and keep you from 'grievance, temptations and venom'. Tales and legends about diamonds abound, including the story of Sinbad and his miraculous escape from the Valley of the Diamonds in *The Book of One Thousand and One Nights.*

In the 1870s, things changed forever when huge quantities of diamonds were discovered in South Africa.

The jewels suddenly became accessible to more than just the supremely wealthy. Companies like De Beers – the world's biggest and most successful diamond company – made their mainly British owners some of the richest men in the world and funded the expansion of the Empire.

In 1947, De Beers employed US advertising agency NW Ayer. They came up with the now iconic phrase 'A diamond is forever', and pushed it so aggressively and successfully that it spawned films, entranced movie stars and became the symbol of love. Diamonds were promoted in the 1950s movie *Gentlemen Prefer Blondes*, starring Marilyn Monroe, who cooed that 'Diamonds are a girl's best friend' – setting the seal on our love affair with the sparkling rocks.

That love affair means big business. In 2004 the market was worth $11.7 billion. Until very recently, women received the rings and men bought them; an old-fashioned way of going about things in a modern world. Young men could spend an average of two months' wages on a diamond engagement ring to prove their love. Now, a new marketing campaign also promotes a diamond ring bought by independent go-getting women. People also buy for same-sex partners. Today, diamonds as 'bling' are the new currency of hip-hop stars, both male and female.

But diamonds also have their dark side. The jewels that sparkle on 100 million fingers, necks and ears have to be mined from the depths of the earth through hard labor. And in 1999 it became clear that ruthless rebels in a number of African countries were using diamonds to buy guns. In the process they were terrorizing and torturing the local populations – as indicated in hip-hop/R&B singer Ms Dynamite's lines: 'Tell me how many Africans died/for the baguettes on your Rolex?' International agencies, the diamond industry and non-governmental organizations moved in to try and control what became

---

## BLING

Bling-bling is a hip-hop phrase meaning expensive jewelry and other accoutrements, and also an entire lifestyle built around excess spending and ostentation. According to the Urban Dictionary, the term originated as Jamaican slang referring to the onomatopoeic 'sound' produced in animated cartoons when light reflects off a diamond. The term was popularized in the US when southern rapper BG used it as the title of his hit song 'Bling-Bling'. The earliest use in a song is DJ Jazzy Jeff and the Fresh Prince using the term in 'Everything That Glitters (Ain't Always Gold)', which was released in 1989 on the album *And In This Corner.* ◆

wikipedia.org

known as 'blood diamonds'. But as it is impossible to detect where a cut diamond has come from, and very easy to smuggle a diamond from one country to another, such controls are still very limited.

We may think of diamonds only as gems, but in fact 80 per cent are used in industry. For hundreds of years, people have been trying to manufacture diamonds. But only recently has it become possible to make a synthetic diamond that is virtually impossible to tell from a real one. Manufactured diamonds are likely to herald a revolution in technology.

But the diamond will always conjure a kind of magic, as long as there's a market for that glittering ring as a symbol of love – and of power and status.

# 1 Genesis of the gem

'Diamonds have nourished men's fantasies
and are synonymous with power, not even
human, but from non-human divine forces.
They are a gift from the Gods.'

PLINY THE ELDER

**There has always been something magical about**
diamonds. They have been associated with wealth
and royalty, with love and loyalty, but also with death
and betrayal. Their early rarity contributed to their
mystique.

The earliest reference comes from northern India, in a
Sanskrit manuscript dated between 320 and 296 BCE. It
was written by Kautiliya, a Minister at the court of King
Chandragupta. It describes the quality of an 'excellent'
diamond as 'big, heavy, capable of bearing blows, with

symmetrical points, capable of scratching a [glass] vessel, revolving like a spindle and brilliantly shining.'

From this period until the 18th century, India was the world's main source of diamonds, although there is some evidence of their use in polishing in China as early as 2,500 BCE. They were traded by land and sea to the east and west, and were sometimes carried off as booty in wars.

Diamonds had already arrived in Rome by the 1st century CE. They are referred to in the writings of Pliny the Elder, who died in 79 CE in the eruption of Mount Vesuvius at Pompeii. In his book *Natural History*, he wrote: 'The substance that possesses the greatest value, not only among precious stones, but of all human possessions, is adamas; a mineral which for a long time was known to kings only, and to very few of them... These stones [diamonds] are tested upon the anvil, and will resist the blow to such an extent as to make the iron rebound and the very anvil split asunder.' Romans were clearly using diamonds for engraving as well. Like Kautiliya, Pliny believed that the stone 'overcomes and neutralizes poisons, dispels delirium, and banishes the groundless perturbations of the mind.'

Archeological digs have never unearthed a diamond,

but holes in ancient jewelry show its 'footprints', round holes with the kind of grooves left by a twin-diamond drill on beads from sites in Yemen dating back to the 4th century BCE. They have also been found in Sri Lanka, India, Thailand, and Egypt.

Diamonds are one of the main features in the 6th-century Indian text, the *Ratnapariksa*. It is a story about a king called Bala, who conquered all his enemies, even the gods. When they could not defeat him, they asked him instead to take part in their sacrificial ritual. He agreed, and was tied to a stake and burned to death. However because he was so pure and noble, his bones were turned into the seeds of gems. These were then plundered by flying creatures, which in their flight dropped them into the oceans, the mountains and the forests, where they

### WHAT'S IN A NAME?

It is likely that the name 'diamond' originally came from the Greek adjective *adamas*, (μ) which meant 'the hardest known substance', as in 'adamant'. No one quite knows when this came to mean a diamond. A version of the word 'diamond' is used in almost every language. In Sanskrit, a diamond is a *vajra*, thunderbolt of the Hindu warrior god Indra. Early descriptions of *vajra* date to the 4th century BCE. ◆

## HARD FACTS

◆ Diamonds were first found in India over 4,000 years ago.

◆ A 13th-century French law proclaimed that only the king could wear diamonds.

◆ Until 1477, when Archduke Maximilian of Austria gave a diamond ring to Mary of Burgundy, only men wore diamonds.

◆ The gems are mined in about 25 countries and on every continent except Europe and Antarctica.

◆ 80 per cent of diamonds mined are used in industry. Only 20 per cent are turned into gems.

◆ The main diamond-producing countries are Russia, Botswana, the Democratic Republic of Congo, Australia, South Africa, Canada, Angola, Namibia, Ghana, Brazil, Sierra Leone and the Central African Republic.

◆ Until 2002, between 4 and 15 per cent of diamonds came from conflict areas. They are known as 'blood diamonds' and it is still almost impossible to say for certain where a diamond comes from, despite an internationally agreed system to control them, called the Kimberley Process.

◆ Americans buy approximately 50 per cent of the world's diamond jewelry.

◆ A diamond's weight is measured in carats, a unit of measurement equal to 200 milligrams. A carat is a fifth of a gram. ◆

grew into precious jewels.

The text goes on to describe the virtues of a diamond; what makes the best stone, its powers and virtues, and distribution among the different Hindu castes. It says: 'The gems and the metals that exist on earth are all scratched by the diamond: the diamond is not (scratched) by them. A noble substance scratches that which is noble and that which is not; the diamond scratches even the ruby. The diamond scratches all and is not scratched by any.' It says that a perfect diamond can be a force for good, bringing 'happiness, prosperity, children, riches, grain, cows and meat'. And a protection against harm: 'He who wears [such] a diamond will see dangers recede from him whether he be threatened by serpents, fire, poison, sickness, thieves, flood or evil spirits.' The magical properties of the gem as a talisman are clearly outlined.

## Abode of the gods

Diamonds were so beautiful that they were considered by many to be the abode of the gods. They were used to decorate religious icons and were thought to bring good fortune to those who owned them. The Hindu caste system originally extended even to the possession of diamonds – only kings were allowed to wear all colors. Brahmins (priests) were allowed to wear white or colorless stones; Kshatriyas (warriors) were allowed to wear brown or red; Vashiyas (landowners), yellow, Shudras (laborers and artisans) grey or black. It goes without saying that those with no caste – outcastes, or Dalits, as they are now known, were not permitted jewels at all. Diamonds also became a Buddhist symbol of spiritual virtue. Tibetan Buddhism is known as the *Vajrayana* (Diamond Vehicle) and the *Diamond Sutra* is one of the most popular texts. The Greeks believed that diamonds were celestial tears; the Romans that they were splinters of fallen stars.

### Indian jewels

It was not until the 13th and 14th centuries that diamonds became a significant commodity in Europe. Venice was the first diamond trading capital. The gems were traded to Antwerp and Bruges in Belgium, and Paris, France. When in 1499 the Portuguese Vasco da Gama sailed round the Cape of Good Hope at the tip of Africa, he opened up another route for traders, centered on Goa in India, which at that time was ruled by Portugal.

In India, diamond production increased during the 300 years of the Moghul Empire from 1526 to 1857. Many beautiful artifacts were decorated with diamonds, and one the world's most famous gems, the Koh-i-noor, dates from this period.

## Europe in the Middle Ages

In most of Europe, however, diamonds were little used for a thousand years after the rise of Christianity. This was partly because the early Christians associated them with idolatry, and partly for practical reasons – Arab and Persian traders restricted the flow of trade between India and Europe.

The Middle Ages saw a growing interest in gemstones in Europe, with many texts, known as 'lapidaries' examining their different qualities and their uses as medicines or poisons. As in earlier times, it was believed that diamonds had protective and curative powers. It was said that a diamond held in the mouth would correct the bad habits of liars and scolds.

Diamonds were worn as talismans against poisoning. Here is a description by Marbode, Bishop of Rennes in France between 1061 and 1081: 'This stone has aptitude for magical arts, indomitable virtues it provides the bearer, nocturnal spirits and bad dreams it repels, black poisons flee, disputes and screams are changed. Cures insanity, strikes hard against enemies. For these purposes the stone should be set in silver, armored in gold, and

## THE MOUNTAIN OF LIGHT

'Koh-i-noor' means 'mountain of light'. The diamond was found in India many thousands of years ago. It entered the history books in the 14th century when it was owned by the Malwa rajas. In 1526, it became the property of Baber, founder of the Moghul Empire, and it belonged to the Moghuls for almost 200 years.

In 1739, King Nadir Shah of Persia invaded India. He captured the Moghuls' treasures, but not the famous diamond, which he was told was hidden in the Emperor's turban. He then devised a plan; he invited the Emperor to a feast and publicly asked to exchange turbans as a gesture of friendship.

The Emperor had to agree or lose face. Instead he lost the diamond, which remained in Persian hands, despite many attempts to wrest it from them – the most gruesome of which was the torture of Nadir Shah's son, Shah Rukh. His eyes were put out, and boiling pitch was poured on his head, but he refused to reveal its hiding place. Finally, one of his descendants

fastened to the left arm.' His treatise was written in Latin and translated into French, Italian, Spanish, Irish, Danish and Hebrew. Lapidaries continued to be written until the 18th century.

Diamonds held a fascination for alchemists, who believed they could turn base metals into gold and fled with the stone to the Punjab, where it was placed in the treasury in Lahore – and then apparently lost.

In 1849, the British retrieved the gem and presented it to Queen Victoria to mark the British East India Company's 250th anniversary. It even turned up in the British TV series Dr Who in April 2006, when *Dr Who* met Queen Victoria, and the gem had been cut to fit into a contraption that looked like a telescope to repel evil spirits and save the Queen's life.

The Koh-i-noor was displayed in the Great Exhibition of 1851. Queen Victoria had it re-cut, reducing the weight from 186 to 108.93 carats. In 1911, it was used in a crown made for Queen Mary, and in 1937, in another for Queen Elizabeth at the coronation of her husband, King George VI.

Since then, many people, including the Taliban in Afghanistan – who claimed that it originally belonged to their country – have tried to get it back. But to this day it remains in the Tower of London as part of the British Crown Jewels. ◆

common things into ones of value. In 1366 Sir John Mandeville said he grew large diamonds from smaller ones: 'I have oftentimes tried the experiment that is a man keep with them a little rock and water them with May dew often, they shall grow every year and the small will grow great.'

## RHODES: DIAMOND DIGGER AND EMPIRE BUILDER

Cecil John Rhodes was born in 1853 in England. He was sent to join his brother in Natal, South Africa, because his lungs were weak. He invested the £3,000 he was given to take with him in diamond claims. It was just at the beginning of the diamond rush and Rhodes went on to become not only one of the richest men in South Africa, but also Prime Minister of the Cape. His views on black and white people served to lay the foundations of apartheid: 'We have got to treat the natives where they are in a state of barbarism, in a different way to ourselves. We are to be lords over them.'

He used his position to consolidate his holdings and to buy out his main rival, Barney Barnato, presenting him with the largest check ever written, for £5,338,650 (about $9 million at current rates). Rhodes then went on to form the De Beers Company, named after the De Beer brothers whose farm had diamonds. But in 1895 he supported an attack – known as the Jameson Raid – on Paul Kruger's Afrikaner Transvaal state. When the raid failed, Rhodes was forced to resign as premier. He used his wealth to expand the British Empire to Rhodesia (now Zimbabwe and Zambia) and to found the Rhodes scholarships, which enabled foreign nationals (including Bill Clinton, who went on to become president of the US) to study in Oxford. Rhodes died in 1902 at the age of 49. ◆

## Rings and royalty

As in India, diamonds were associated with wealth and status. In Europe, royalty and nobles started to use diamonds along with the pearls that they bedecked themselves with in the 13th century. Louis IX of France, who ruled from 1214 to 1270, decreed that diamonds were only to be used by the King. It was not until 1477, when Archduke Maximilian of Austria gave a diamond ring to Mary of Burgundy, that diamonds became more widely worn by women as a symbol of love.

Cosimo the Elder in Italy (1389-1464) and Henry II of France (1519-59) placed diamonds in rings and wore them into battle for good luck. François I of France and Henry VIII of England, who both ruled in the first half of the 16th century, competed to show off the best jewels. By the 17th century lesser mortals such as wealthy merchants began to use them in their jewelry.

## Diamonds around the world

Until this time, India was the main source of diamonds. However in 1725 gold miners found diamonds in Brazil, and from 1730 until 1870, Brazil became the world's major source of diamonds. Then, in 1870, huge deposits were discovered in South Africa. The subsequent rush and the

## THE SECOND WORLD WAR

Diamonds were part of the power struggle between countries as well as individuals and companies. During the Second World War, they were smuggled from Africa to Germany. Control of diamonds, including industrial diamonds, was seen as being of vital importance by both sides. During the early years of the War, industrial diamonds were in short supply in the British aircraft industry and the Canadian mining industry. Germany had been stockpiling diamonds in preparation for war since 1936, and continued to import them from Brazil and Venezuela. It acquired large stockpiles when it invaded Belgium and took over Antwerp in May 1940. The British and American governments argued over diamonds, as the US initially refused to prohibit exports to Germany and wanted to buy Britain's stocks in case Britain fell into German hands. But after Pearl Harbor, a compromise agreement was reached and stockpiles established in Canada. ◆

richness of the seams changed the face of the diamond world forever. It meant that diamonds were no longer so rare. By 1871, world annual production exceeded a million carats for the first time, thanks mainly to the South African finds.

The discovery took place in 1866, when a 15-year-old Afrikaner called Erasmus Jacobs was working on his father's farm, near Kimberley: 'In the glare of the strong sun [I saw] a glittering pebble some yards away... I of course had no idea that the stone was of value... After reaching home I handed the mooi klip (pretty pebble) to my younger sister, who simply placed it among her playthings.' A visiting neighbor, Schalk van Niekerk noticed the stone and Erasmus's mother gave it to him as a present. He sold it to a trader called Jack O'Reilly for a few pounds. It was not until the stone was examined by surgeon and amateur mineralogist, Dr Guybon Atherstone, that he recognized it for what it was – a 21.25 carat diamond.

The news spread, and soon there was a diamond rush around the Orange (Gariep) River. By 1869, as diamonds in that area ran out, desperate men searched further afield, first in soft earth and later, in the town of Kimberley, in volcanic rock known because of its color as 'blueground'. This would later be given the name kimberlite. For the next 15 years, the area around Kimberley went on to produce 95 per cent of the world's diamonds, in quantities never seen before.

The mines were ruled by British emigrant families who were to be made famous (and wealthy) by diamonds: Cecil Rhodes, Barney Barnato, and their company, De Beers. Black miners did the digging in their mines while whites, who earned many times more, were the overseers. The mining industry worked to create and then consolidate the separate systems for blacks and whites that became known as apartheid. Lord Randolph Churchill, father of Winston and then Chancellor of the Exchequer, noted on a visit to Kimberley that black miners 'have to strip off all their clothes... stark naked, they then proceed to the searching room, where their mouths, their hair, their toes, their armpits, and every portion of their body are subject to an elaborate examination.' He added that white men 'would never submit to such a process, but the native sustains the indignity with cheerful equanimity.'

Today, De Beers' seven mines in South Africa still produce 97 per cent of the country's diamond output. The company continues to dominate the diamond industry.

# 2 Diamonds in the rough

'Its color is that of ice, and as the dew drop or drop of water from a mountain stream sparkles in the light of the sun, as the icicle sparkles.'

GEORGE FREDERICK KUNZ, AUTHOR AND DIAMOND EXPERT.

**What do we know about diamonds? They are** expensive, they are beautiful, they sparkle. They are found underground. They are the some of the oldest things on earth. And they are the hardest substance known to humans. But what are diamonds made of? And what is it that makes them so precious, so expensive, and unique among gems?

Diamonds are made of carbon, the stuff of life. While other gems are also carbon, it is a diamond's crystal

## WHY DIAMONDS ARE UNIQUE

◆ According to a scale developed by German scientist Friedrich Mohs in 1812, a diamond has a hardness of 1,500. The next hardest mineral is corundum at 400, then topaz at 200 and quartz at 100.

◆ A diamond can be cut along four different lines and does not shatter or fragment.

◆ A diamond's surface repels water but accepts wax and grease, making it easy to separate from other matter.

◆ Because a diamond is formed under high pressure, its atoms are squeezed more tightly together than other gems, making it very dense. The pressure that formed a diamond was equivalent to the Eiffel Tower resting upside down on a five-inch plate.

◆ Diamonds sparkle because their high density enables them to bend or slow (refract) light to the maximum extent possible as it passes through the gem. Some can even change color.

◆ Not all diamonds are colorless – they can be pink, blue, yellow or violet or even black. Yellow comes from the addition of nitrogen, blue from boron. Some of the most valuable ones are colored. A colorless diamond is pure carbon.

◆ Kiss a diamond, and it feels cold on your lips – probably why they have been nicknamed 'ice'.

◆ There are even glow-in-the-dark diamonds. Some are fluorescent under ultra violet light because they can absorb high-energy radiation and send it out again as visible light. ◆

structure that makes it so special. A crystal is formed from the bonding of atoms in a repeating pattern. In a carbon atom, four of its six electrons can bond with other atoms. A diamond is unique in that all four of these atoms make such a bond, while graphite, for example, only has three atoms that bond in this way. This is what makes a diamond hard and graphite soft, and gives the diamond many of its other unique qualities, such as its 'cleavage'; how a diamond can be cut cleanly by another diamond, rather than fragmenting into small or jagged pieces.

Diamonds are the hardest substance on earth, 750 times harder than a fingernail and 300 times harder than a steel file. Only a diamond can cut another diamond.

**Star dust**

Most diamonds are estimated to be three billion years old, three-quarters of the age of the earth. Some younger ones are only 100 million years old. Most were created in molten rock, 75 to 120 miles below the earth's surface and then blown to the surface in volcanic eruptions through 'pipes' of volcanic rock known as kimberlite. Diamonds are often found with other minerals, such as garnet, chromite, ilmenite, clinopyroxene, olivine, and zircon. Sometimes these minerals can actually be embedded in

## GLOWING GEMS

The Emperor of Brazil, Pedro II de Alcantara, a descendant of the Austrian Hapsburgs and the Portuguese Braganzas, ruled Brazil from 1831 to 1889. He was interested in diamonds, mineral specimens, and geology. He gave a 2.15-carat diamond to his niece that glowed greenish yellow in fluorescent light or daylight and turned yellowish brown in incandescent light. ◆

the diamond. All are indicators to diamond diggers of the presence of diamonds in the rock.

The Romans were not far wrong when they said that diamonds come from star dust. Diamonds are found where meteorites have hit the earth with huge impact at immense pressure. Meteorites themselves can contain diamonds, and the most ancient contain remnants of the death of stars, some of which is tiny bits of diamond older than the solar system itself. In February 2004, astronomers discovered a white dwarf star that has a 3,000-kilometer wide core of crystallized carbon – a diamond of ten billion trillion trillion carats. They have called it Lucy, after the Beatles' song 'Lucy in the Sky with Diamonds'.

Today, diamonds are found and mined in about 25 countries and on every continent except Europe and Antarctica. In the latter, international agreements

# WHERE DIAMONDS ARE FOUND

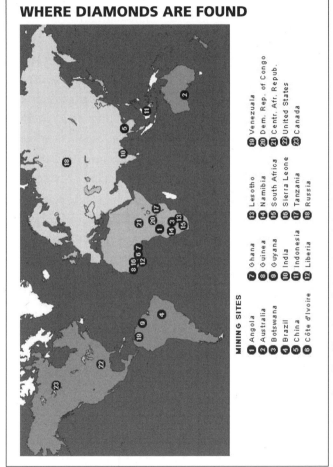

**MINING SITES**

1 Angola
2 Australia
3 Botswana
4 Brazil
5 China
6 Côte d'Ivoire
7 Ghana
8 Guinea
9 Guyana
10 India
11 Indonesia
12 Liberia
13 Lesotho
14 Namibia
15 South Africa
16 Sierra Leone
17 Tanzania
18 Russia
19 Venezuela
20 Dem. Rep. of Congo
21 Centr. Afr. Repub.
22 United States
23 Canada

http://americanradioworks.publicradio.org/features/diamonds/facts/html

29

prohibit mining. In India, the Majhgawan pipe in the north is now the only producing source of diamonds. South Africa has been a major producer since the 1870s. Australia discovered diamonds in 1979 on the aptly-named Kimberley Plateau in Western Australia. And it was as recently as 1991 that diamonds were discovered in Canada's Northwest Territories. Other major mining countries are Botswana, Russia, and the Democratic Republic of the Congo (DRC). Africa accounts for about 53 per cent of world production. There are only two sources of diamonds in the US – in Arkansas and Colorado. In Arkansas, the mine is part of a State Park, and you can dig for the gems for $5.00 – though you are unlikely to find anything. Colorado is the only operating diamond mine in America.

## Diamond mining

There are two types of diamond deposits, known as primary and secondary sources. Primary sources are those which bring diamonds up from the earth's rocky mantle, like kimberlite. Secondary sources are created by erosion, near pipes, in streams, rivers and on beaches.

It takes 8 years on average between discovering a deposit and opening a mine. First you have to ensure that there are enough diamonds to make it worthwhile by bulk sampling, raising the money, feasibility studies, reviewing environmental impact, obtaining permits and building the mine and its infrastructure.

**Digging the land...**

Mining a kimberlite pipe starts by digging a hole into the pipe. This is known as 'open-pit' or 'open-cast' mining. Loose material is taken out by hydraulic shovels, while hard rock is drilled and blasted. If the pipe proves to be full of diamonds, then it is time to explore further by sinking shafts and digging tunnels. This can now be done mechanically, but in the past (and in some countries this is still the case) the material had to be dug out by men in very dangerous conditions. In a De Beers mine, on average, 250 tons of ore would need to be excavated to find a stone that would be big enough to polish into a one-carat diamond.

Once they have been brought to the surface, diamonds have to be separated from the earth and rocks. In the past, this would be by means of a washing pan: diamonds fell to the bottom because they are heavier than the other material. Today, a more mechanical version of the same technique is used in many mines. Diamonds will stick to grease and wax and these can still be used as part of the

> ### KIMBERLEY KIMBERLITE
>
> Kimberlites are the most important source of primary diamonds. Many kimberlite 'pipes' also produce rich alluvial or eluvial diamond placer deposits.
>
> The deposits occurring at Kimberley, South Africa were the first recognized and hence the source of the name. ◆

http://en.wikipedia.org

process. The final separation and sorting often still has to be done by eye.

### Panning the rivers...

Originally, many diamonds were discovered in secondary sources, in riverbeds or streams and even fossilized rivers. In some countries, such as Sierra Leone, people still use the oldest methods, panning for diamonds or using shovels and buckets. More sophisticated operations use large earth-moving equipment.

### Searching the seas...

The diamonds that survive a pounding by the oceans tend to be very good grade and so make it worth the cost of searching the seas. Marine mining can be done in three ways. First on land, by moving sand from 10 meters below sea level to see what there is on the bedrock. Second, using

## WORLD DIAMOND PRODUCTION 2004

(millions of carats)

| Top 12 | Millions of carats |
| --- | --- |
| Russia | 35,000 |
| Botswana | 31,125 |
| DR Congo | 29,000 |
| Australia | 20,673 |
| South Africa | 14,233 |
| Canada | 12,618 |
| Angola | 7,500 |
| Namibia | 2,011 |
| Ghana | 900 |
| Brazil | 700 |
| Sierra Leone | 600 |
| Central African Republic | 500 |
| **World total** | **156,127** |

Source: De Beers, Rio Tinto, BHP Billiton, quoted in www.iti.gove.nt.ca/diamond/industry.htm

divers with suction pipes in up to 20 meters of water. Third, using deep-sea boats with remote underwater tractors or large underwater excavators.

### Diamonds and the environment

The gems unearthed may sparkle, but diamond mines do little to make the surrounding environment more beautiful. Having displaced the people who live there –

Janine Robert's book *Glitter and Greed* cites examples of Aboriginal and San land and sacred sites being taken over – they create large pits in the ground, sometimes many hundreds of meters deep and wide. Once the diamonds have been plundered, gaping holes are just left as deep scars on the landscape.

In Kimberley, South Africa, tourists now come to see 'The Big Hole' – a diamond mine covering 170,000 square meters and 800 meters deep which was abandoned in 1914 and filled with water. The Canadian Arctic Resources Committee cites the following impacts of the two diamond mines operating in the Northwest Territories of Canada: 'Loss of fish habitat through draining of lakes, destruction of streams, changes in water quality. Water quality changes are measurable as far as 200 km downstream of Lac de Gras (Ekati mine), and there have been irreversible changes to water quality and possibly species composition in Snap Lake (De Beers diamond project). Twenty lakes have been eliminated altogether, with no fish habitat compensation measures in place.'

**From mine to dealer**

When diamonds come from the mines, they appear battered and dirty, sometimes compared to 'lumps of washing soda'. Before they can be sold to a dealer, they first have to be cleaned and sorted into three categories: gem-quality, near gem-quality, and industrial-grade diamonds. At the mine, diamonds are grouped into sizes:

◆ More than one carat – diamonds larger than 15 carats are handled individually into different shapes such as 'stones', 'shapes', 'cleavages', 'macles' and 'flats'.

◆ 'Smalls' – between one carat and one-tenth of a carat

◆ 'Sands' – less than one-tenth of a carat.

Once sorted, there is still a long way to go before a diamond ends up as jewelry. They have to be cut, polished and graded according to what is known in the trade as 'The Four Cs':

◆ Carat  ◆ Cut  ◆ Color  ◆ Clarity


## 1 Carat

A carat is the measurement used to weigh a diamond. The term comes from the word *carubis*, the seed of the carob tree (native to the Mediterranean region) that were once used to balance weighing scales. One carat is 0.2 grams or about 0.007 ounces. Carats are divided further into points. The higher the number of carats, the more valuable the diamond.

## 2 Cut

*'First I told myself I must achieve the essence of beauty... the stone allowed me to dream of other angles, other refractions of light... it was as if the stone looked at me... and when I began shaping, it revealed itself more and more.'*

Gabi Tolkowsky, great nephew of Marcel (see below) and cutter of the 599-carat Centenary Diamond, found in 1986.

The cut of a diamond is crucial to its value. The cutting and polishing of a diamond results in a dramatic loss of weight – often more than 50 per cent – while at the same time the stone's value increases by up to 40 per cent. Sometimes cutters try to preserve the carat rating at the cost of the cut; this is particularly true for diamonds of around one carat, because a one-carat diamond is more valuable than one just a little smaller. Cutting is a very skilled trade and it can take months to determine the right way to cleave a diamond. Trained diamond cutters can command 6-figure salaries.

A cut diamond usually has 57 facets, and a good cut will give the diamond extra sparkle. There are mathematical guidelines for cutting to reflect the maximum amount of light. These date back to 1919 when Belgian mathematician Marcel Tolkowsky developed an ideal cut with 33 facets on the top half, or crown, and 24 on the lower half, known as the 'pavilion'. He specified the angles and percentages of each. The point at the bottom of the diamond is known as a 'culet'. Often a thin girdle around the middle is needed to prevent chipping.

There are a range of different cuts apart from the traditional round one. They include emerald cuts, marquise, pear, brilliant, rose and drop, as well as cuts in the shape of different flowers.

### 3 Color

Diamonds are not just 'white' or colorless. They come in a whole range of colors. Generally, colorless diamonds are more valuable, but colored diamonds (known in the industry as 'fancy' diamonds), are currently very fashionable – Jennifer Lopez/J-Lo's engagement ring was a large pink diamond. The price of a diamond depends on its color; the rarer it is, the greater the cost.

The Gemological Institute of America (GIA) uses a D to Z scale it developed for grading the color of white diamonds, where D is colorless and Z is yellow:

◆ colorless: D, E, F

◆ near colorless: G, H, I, J

◆ faint yellow or brown: K, L, M

♦ very light yellow or brown: N, O, P, Q, R
♦ light yellow or brown: S, T, U, V, W, X, Y, Z

## 4 Clarity

The clarity of a diamond is about its internal defects, known as inclusions. These might be crystals or tiny cracks. A grading system for clarity is based on the inclusions visible to a trained professional looking at a diamond that is magnified 10 times. The grade is on a scale from 'flawless' to 'imperfect'.

### 'Diamond mining is bad for your health'

Being a diamond miner can be bad for your health. The rock within the diamond pipe sometimes contains asbestos. One miner told writer Janine Roberts: 'Dust is

| COST PER CARAT, SEPTEMBER 2005 | |
|---|---|
| Carat size | Cost per carat $ |
| 0.5 carat (50 points) | 3,000 |
| 1.0 carat | 6,500 |
| 1.5 carats | 8,500 |
| 2.0 carats | 13,000 |
| 3.0 carats | 17,000 |
| 5.0 carats | 23,000 |

everywhere... it blocks our noses with black stuff despite our flimsy nosebags [dust masks]. It is especially bad when mixed with the fumes from blasting.' Many workers have lung and breathing problems. And regular X-rays to check that no miner is stealing a diamond may well have effects that have still not been monitored.

Diamond-cutting can also be a health hazard. The Indian Government lists the diamond industry as one of its 'top ten hazardous industries '. The cutting tools create dust, and many children are still employed in the industry there, despite attempts to ban this practice.

## Uses of diamonds

Eighty per cent of diamonds are used in industry – only 20 per cent are used as gems. Diamonds have three main uses in industry: as cutting tools, as abrasives, and as powder or paste for grinding and polishing. It may be expensive, but a diamond is so effective and long-lasting that it is worth the expense. And because its hardness means it does not wear down, it can continue to cut in exactly the same way for ever. The only thing a diamond cannot be used for is to cut iron, because of a high-temperature reaction between iron and carbon.

Diamond machine tools are used for turning, milling

## THE CUTTING OF THE GREAT STAR OF AFRICA

The Great Star of Africa was cut from the Cullinan (see p 45), the largest diamond ever found. The story goes that it was sent to Amsterdam to be cut by expert diamond cutters, the Asscher brothers. It took them months to decide on the right cut. Finally they were ready. On the first cut, the blade broke. On the second, the diamond split as planned – and one of the brothers fainted clean away. Luckily he had a doctor and a nurse on hand, just in case... ◆

and boring plastics, glass, and metals. They can cut, grind and polish stones, ceramics, metals and concrete. The industrial uses of diamonds include:

◆ Shaping drums for copying machines
◆ Polygon mirrors in laser printers
◆ Aluminum-alloy pistons in car engines
◆ Eye glasses
◆ Computer chips
◆ Blades, especially for surgical use
◆ Phonograph needles
◆ Drill bits used in drilling for oil, water or natural gas.

# 3 Money matters

'The moment De Beers Consolidated Mines was incorporated by Cecil Rhodes some 110 years ago it became the largest and most successful diamond company in the world, and so it has remained. I always feel longevity must mean we are doing something right and fulfilling a need.'

NICKY OPPENHEIMER, CHAIR OF DE BEERS, IN 1999.

**We are buying more diamonds every year. And they** are seriously big business. In 2004, world diamond production was worth $11.7 billion, an increase from $9.1 billion in 2003. Forecasts for 2008 are almost $14 billion.

Canada has gone from seventh to third-largest diamond producer (in value) in the world in just one year. And yet diamonds were only discovered in Canada's Northwest Territories in 1991. Between 1998 and 2002, 13.8 million

DIAMONDS • TRIGGER ISSUES

carats were mined at a value of $2.8 billion. 'This is roughly a 1.5-kilogram bag of ice each day for five years, with each bag worth $1.5 million,' a Statistics Canada paper says. By the end of 2006, there will be four mines running; they are expected to last for another 18 years, even if no more sources are discovered. And they are likely to be: the number of prospecting permits jumped to 1,518 in 2004 from 190 in 2003. It has made some of the mining towns into boom towns – Yellowknife Mayor Dave Lowell said of the diamond rush in his town, 'Quite simply, it is our future. We'd be going into quite a recession if it wasn't for the diamond mine.'

### WORLD DIAMOND PRODUCTION ($ billions)

| Year | Value |
|------|-------|
| 2004 | 11.7 |
| 2003 | 9.4 |
| 2002 | 7.9 |
| 2001 | 7.7 |
| 2000 | 8.0 |
| 1999 | 7.6 |

**The diamond pipeline**

The 'diamond pipeline' refers to the processes through which a diamond goes from the time it is found in the ground to the point of sale. The increase in value from the time a diamond is found in the ground to the moment it sparkles on a finger is phenomenal. In 2004, worldwide retail sales were estimated at $61.5

## TOP 12 DIAMOND-PRODUCING COUNTRIES BY VALUE ($ millions) 2004

The top diamond producing countries in terms of value in 2004 were Botswana, Russia and Canada.

| | |
|---|---:|
| Botswana | 2,940 |
| Russia | 1,989 |
| Canada | 1,646 |
| South Africa | 1,458 |
| Angola | 1,300 |
| DR Congo | 790 |
| Namibia | 698 |
| Australia | 343 |
| Sierra Leone | 200 |
| Central African Republic | 95 |
| Brazil | 35 |
| Ghana | 26 |
| **World total** | **11,777** |

Round    Marquise    Princess    Emerald    Oval    Pear

www.iti.gov.nt.ca/diamond/industry

billion, about five and a half times the value of rough diamond production, and up 8.7 per cent from the previous year. Value is added at each stage, from one purchaser to another, and from rough to polished, to cut diamond. It includes the non-diamond components of a ring or necklace such as precious metals, semiprecious stones, design, distribution, marketing and advertising.

Americans buy half of the world's jewelry diamonds and demand appears to be insatiable. Japan is the second-largest market. In the Middle East and Asia, where there is a burgeoning middle class, people are buying increasing numbers of diamonds – between 2003 and 2004, the Indian market increased by 19 per cent, the Turkish by 25 per cent and the Chinese by 11 per cent. The weakness of the dollar has helped to keep the price of diamonds down, as they are traded in dollars until the point they are sold to the consumer.

Increasingly, diamonds are being sold on the internet. Type 'diamond' into Google, and most sites that come up are about selling you a diamond. Although only two per cent of diamond jewelry sales in the US are made online, this is increasing all the time. Research shows that jewelry

## THE DIAMOND PIPELINE, 2004 ($ billions)

| Rough diamond production | Rough bought for production | Value of polished ex-production | Polished diamond content in retail sales | Retail sales of diamond jewelry |
|---|---|---|---|---|
| 11.7 | 12.1 | 14.8 | 16.7 | 61.5 |

## THE BIGGEST DIAMOND IN THE WORLD

The Cullinan diamond was found in 1905 at the Premier mines in South Africa by Frederick Wells, a mine superintendent. He saw what he thought was a large piece of glass in the wall of the mine. At 3,106 carats, it turned out to be one of the largest diamonds in the world. He was paid $10,000 and the diamond was named after Sir Thomas Cullinan, the mine owner. It was cut into 105 separate diamonds. The largest two were the Great Star of Africa (known as Cullinan I, a 530-carat diamond) and the Lesser Star of Africa (known as the Cullinan II, weighing 317.40 carats). ◆

and watches are the fastest growing internet purchases, up by over 50 per cent between 2003 and 2004.

### De Beers Company

De Beers, the Canadian Aber Diamond company, the Australian-British BHP Billiton, and the British-Australian company Rio Tinto are the largest diamond mining companies. De Beers part-owns Debswana with the Government of Botswana, and part-owns Namdeb with the Namibian Government.

De Beers, the brainchild of Cecil Rhodes, is still the largest diamond company in the world. In 2004, its mines in Botswana, South Africa, Namibia and Tanzania produced an estimated $4.9 billion worth of diamonds – 42 per cent of world production. It also sells around $700 million worth of the output of the Russian State Mining

## ROBBER CAUGHT... BY A SANDWICH

On 16 February 2003, thieves broke into Belgium's famous Antwerp Diamond Center and pulled off one of the country's biggest heists. They plundered 123 of 160 vaults before making off with more than $100 million in gems. Amazingly, the robbery wasn't noticed until the following day.

Less than two weeks after the break-in, the police found an unusual piece of evidence that they believed was linked to the crime; bags in a ditch which contained a partially eaten sandwich, security camera tapes and safe documents. An examination of the tapes and documents revealed that they came from the heist.

Perhaps the most surprising piece of evidence was derived from the half-eaten sandwich, from which police abstracted DNA. The investigation led the police to Leonardo Notarbartolo, 51, a diamond merchant who rented office space in the Antwerp Diamond Center and had been to the vaults on several occasions. Although he was not directly involved in the robbery, he was suspected of links to the robbers.

None of the diamonds have been found. ◆

Company, Alrosa, which gives it a 48 per cent share in the world diamond market.

If it were any other industry, there might have been mutterings about monopolies, but the system that Cecil Rhodes (pictured left) set up is so flawless that it has kept almost total control over diamond production and diamond sales until very recently. The fact that it controls diamond production and trade was seen as a bonus by Nicky Oppenheimer, chair of De Beers, who was reported in *The Times* in 2002, describing his company as 'the world's longest running monopoly'. He noted that its aim was 'to manage the diamond market, to control supply, to manage prices and to act collusively with our partners in the rural parts of Africa.'

## How the diamond trade works

In 1934 De Beers set up the Diamond Trading Corporation (DTC) to handle rough diamond sales. Together with the Diamond Producers' Association, a group of mine operators, today they form the heart of the Central Selling Organization (CSO), which controls the price of diamonds on the world market and finances mining technology for governments.

Linda Davies, author of the novel *Wilderness of Mirrors* about the diamond trade, says: 'It is a brilliant operation. Over the past 60 years the CSO has done for diamonds something that eluded the oil producers of OPEC and even the cocaine barons of the Medellín cartel. It had the muscle and the nerve to impose its own order on the market, and it built a syndicate not for weeks or months but for decades.'

The Diamond Trading Corporation holds ten selling sessions called 'sights' every year. These are by invitation only, and only a handful of diamond manufacturers, known as 'sightholders' are allowed to attend. The value of each sight varies from $500,000 to $2 million. Sightholders deal with six intermediary brokers, who liaise with De Beers to get the kind of 'parcels' of stones that they need for their clients. De Beers apparently calls this 'feeding the ducks'.

Sightholders may get the diamonds cut themselves, or sell some of the rough diamonds to smaller manufacturers to cut and sell on to jewelry manufacturers (who set the diamonds into finished pieces of jewelry and then sell it to retailers). Or sightholders may sell to wholesalers who then sell to retailers. In the US cartels are illegal, so De Beers is represented by a public relations office, the Diamond Information Center, and indirectly by the diamond dealers and jewelers who sell the gems.

De Beers' share of the market has dropped in recent years. Only 15 years ago, they sold 80 per of the world's rough diamonds. Most of the remainder was traded in Antwerp. In 1996, Rio Tinto Australia's Argyle Mine broke away from the CSO channel and started to sell independently from their office in Antwerp. Others soon followed suit. This was the beginning of major changes for De Beers.

In 1999, in the face of a decline in demand, new sources of competition and the scandal about 'conflict diamonds' (see next chapter), De Beers decided to move the company into the retail business in addition to selling rough diamonds, and to become the 'supplier of choice' – that is, to focus on marketing.

**Forever**

In order to do so, it decided on a new brand. Instead of De Beers, it would use DTC (Diamond Trading Company), with a new icon, known as the ForeverMark based on the original 'A diamond is forever' slogan, and its own glitzy website. At the same time, it increased its advertising budget to $200 million and went into partnership with luxury brand company LVMH, which owns brands such as Louis Vuitton, Givenchy, Fendi, Christian Dior, and TAG Heuer. In 2001 De Beers was bought out by Anglo-American and the Oppenheimer family, delisting from the Johannesburg Stock Exchange (JSE) after more than 100 years. The business was valued at $9.3 billion at buy-out.

Meanwhile, the De Beers Company continues to invest in looking for new sources of diamonds in countries like Brazil, China and Canada. In 2004 it spent $111 million on exploration. Its mines in Canada are likely to produce a billion dollars' worth of diamonds by 2015. And its rough diamond sales in 2004 were $5.7 billion, a 3 per cent increase over 2003.

## Polishing, cutting and trading

For many years Antwerp in Belgium was the main diamond-polishing center in the world, as well as the place where rough diamonds were imported and traded. It is no longer a major polishing center, though around 1,500 polishers still cut the more valuable rough stones.

Many factories in Russia, China and the Far East are owned by Belgian companies and managed by Belgian technicians.

Jewish refugees in Israel set up polishing businesses after the Second World War. Today, Israeli companies own polishing factories in the Far East, Russia and China. Sixty-seven per cent of Israel's polished diamonds are exported to the US and they are worth $2.1 billion.

Over the past 30 years, India has taken over from Belgium and Israel as the dominant polishing center. In 2004, it imported a net $6.9 billion of rough diamonds, and exported polished diamonds with a net value of $8.4 billion. This is more than half the estimated world total output of polished diamonds. Originally, India worked with low-quality stones but today it polishes all types. The workforce involved is estimated at 700,000 people and has all the latest technology. Officially, child labor in the diamond industry is banned, but in the late 1990s a European Union investigation found 6-year old children in diamond workshops, many trapped there by debt bondage.

Russia has been polishing and cutting diamonds since Soviet times and now has the largest manufacturing industry of any diamond-producing country. Polished diamond output is estimated at $800 million a year. In China, over the past five years the diamond workforce has grown from 11,000 to a current 25,000, working in about 80 polishing companies. They cut mostly small, gem-quality stones.

New centers for polishing are being developed in New

---

## NAIL-BITING SECURITY

In March 2005 Holland's biggest-ever diamond raid took place at Amsterdam's Schiphol Airport after thieves hijacked a security truck with jewels worth around 75 million euros ($99.10 million).

Industry organization Aircargo Nederland (ACN) said the robbery came as no surprise given that military police have been told to concentrate on fighting drug smuggling, human trafficking and preventing attacks.

Michel Einhorn of Cool Diamonds, who said he lost $1.2 million worth of gems in the theft, told Dutch daily *Algemeen Dagblad* he did not expect them to be found and criticized security at the airport.

'An airport is supposed to be amongst the most impenetrable places of the land. It is unthinkable that armed men entered the terrain and then left without a shot being fired. And I cannot even pass security with a nail clipper,' he added. ◆

news.airwtraise.com

---

York, Armenia, Thailand and Sri Lanka. There is a trend towards polishing in the countries where diamonds originate. South Africa, Namibia, Angola, Canada and Botswana are all developing their own polishing centers. In Canada, the Government will only allow a diamond mine to open if the stones are polished and cut in the country so that the added value remains within the nation.

## Polar bear

These diamonds have a tiny polar bear engraved on them. Diamonds not only make millions for those who trade in them, they also provide many jobs and prop up whole economies. In Botswana, the world's largest diamond-producer by value, the gems account for 75 per cent of the country's annual foreign exchange earnings, 65 per cent of government revenue and 35 per cent of its gross domestic product. In Namibia, the diamond industry is the country's largest employer and exports account for 40 per cent of its foreign exchange earnings. In South Africa, 50 per cent of De Beers' mining profits go to the Government and more than 11,000 people are employed in the diamond industry.

Diamonds constitute the most important export of the

Central African Republic, accounting for 40 to 55 per cent of export revenues, although large quantities are smuggled out illegally. In India, more than a million people are employed in the cutting and polishing industry.

## Sensational heists

The fact that diamonds are tiny and valuable also makes them easy pickings for thieves. They have been the target in some of the world's most audacious heists.

◆  In  1953,  Sir  Ernest  Oppenheimer  of  De  Beers

---

### THE HOPE DIAMOND

The Hope is a 44-carat blue diamond once owned by Louis XIV of France. It was stolen during the French Revolution and disappeared. It changed hands several times over the next two centuries, finding its way into the possession of Henry Philip Hope, one of the heirs of the British banking firm Hope & Co, in the 1830s. In 1909 it wound up with Pierre Cartier of the Cartier jewelry empire, before landing in the US. It has a reputation for bad luck; all the Hope family died penniless, as did another owner, Edward McLean. In 1830, the man who cut the diamond reportedly committed suicide after his son stole the jewel. And according to legend, an actress was shot on stage the first night she wore the famous gem.

It was donated to the US Smithsonian Institution in 1958. ◆

---

approached former head of the British M15, Sir Percy Sillitoe, to help combat trafficking in diamonds. Sir Percy agreed, and after visiting diamond mines all over Africa set up the International Diamond Security Organization which had the twin aims of increasing security at the mines and revealing the major channels of smuggling to Europe, the Middle East, and the former Soviet Union. This was disbanded in 1957 as it was thought it had achieved its aims.

◆ In 1999 there was an almost successful attempt to steal $200 millions worth of diamonds from an exhibition in London's Millennium Dome. Robbers had planned a James Bond-style escape in a boat along the river Thames.

◆ In February 2003, thieves broke into Belgium's Antwerp Diamond Center and pulled off one of the world's biggest heists. They plundered 123 of 160 vaults before making off with more than $100 million in gems. The diamonds have never been found.

◆ In scenes worthy of Dan Brown's novel, *The Da Vinci Code,* thieves stole two diamonds worth more than $13 million from a display case at a Paris antique show near the Louvre in September 2004.

◆ In February 2005, two men dressed as KLM workers

---

**A DIAMOND IN THE ROUGH
OR 'ROUGH DIAMOND'**
♦ An unpolished or inexperienced person who shows promise.

---

entered the cargo terminal of Amsterdam's Schiphol
Airport in a stolen KLM car. The men intercepted a truck
carrying millions of dollars' worth of diamonds, which
were on route to a Tulip Air plane bound for Antwerp.
♦ Also in 2005 London's Natural History Museum closed
its diamond exhibition because of police advice that there
was a 'heightened criminal risk'.

# 4 The dark behind the dazzle

'The symbol of love and happiness in America should not be paid for with the blood of Africans.'
US DEMOCRATIC SENATOR DICK DURBIN.

**It is a strange contradiction that many of the stones** sold in the name of love are dug out of the ground with blood, sweat and tears. Those who sell the diamonds are anxious to keep such connections as far apart as possible, but in the late 1990s a number of unpleasant facts began to surface about the source of certain diamonds and their role in the international arms trade.

These diamonds, sometimes known as 'conflict diamonds' or 'blood diamonds' were estimated to be worth between 4 and 15 per cent of the total trade in rough diamonds. Smuggling diamonds is nothing new. There can be few things so valuable that are as small, as easily portable and as difficult to detect. In the early days, this was one of the reasons why black mineworkers were forced to live in compounds, so that they could not smuggle anything out at the end of a day's work.

In his 1948 book, *The Heart of the Matter*, set in Sierra Leone, Graham Greene describes diamonds being smuggled in the stomachs of live parrots. In the early 1950s, tens of millions of dollars of diamonds were being smuggled out of Africa every year. Ian Fleming's James Bond story, *Diamonds are Forever*, has the gems smuggled in golf balls. *Blood Diamonds* by Greg Campbell describes

a prominent British diamond merchant who smuggled $2 million worth of polished diamonds from London to Belgium over a three-year period. He was only caught when somebody stole $184,000 of the cache from him. The most remarkable thing was that he had been on Her Majesty's Customs

Agency for 11 years as part of their diamond evaluation committee. And it is not just individuals either: between 1993 and 1997, Guinea reported official sales of 2.6 million carats to Belgium, while Belgium reported imports of nearly twice that amount.

In 1998, the non-governmental organization Global Witness (GW) blew the whistle on how the diamond trade in Angola was propping up the conflict there. Its report 'Rough trade: the role of diamond companies and governments in the Angolan conflict' documented how the diamond trade funded the rebel UNITA movement and the consequences of this for the people of Angola. Angola's civil war left half a million dead and 86 000 maimed. UNITA controlled 60-70 per cent of the diamond trade, generating $3.7 billion in diamonds.

## Blood diamonds

The report stated that: 'UNITA's diamonds reach the major international markets through a worldwide diamond industry that operates with little transparency or scrutiny from the international community'. It warned that 'there is a dangerous acceptance amongst the international community that the mechanics of the trade in diamonds, particularly from the UNITA-controlled areas, are beyond

## THE STORY OF JUSU LAHIA

In April 2001, when Jusu Lahia was 15 years old, he was wounded by an exploding rocket-propelled grenade. A lieutenant in Sierra Leone's Revolutionary United Front (RUF), Lahia was picked off during a battle. He was among thousands of victims of a war fought for control of one of the world's most precious commodities: a fortune in raw diamonds that have made their way from the deadly jungles of Sierra Leone onto the rings and necklaces of happy lovers the world over.

While Lahia sprawled on the earth – shards of hot metal ripped his body from face to groin, destroying his left eye – few who eventually wore the gems he fought over could even locate Sierra Leone on the map.

Lahia was carried to a bare, fire-blackened hospital room in Kailahun, the RUF's stronghold. When I first saw him there, surrounded by chaos, heat and filth, I found it hard to remember that the cause of all this suffering – thousands of doomed refugees, well-armed but illiterate and drugged combatants, fallen wounded like Lahia, and injured civilian children – was brutally simple: the greed for diamonds. Certainly, there was nothing nearly as lustrous or awe-inspiring as a diamond in the blood-stained room where Lahia was dying of a tetanus infection, next to another felled 15 year-old. Powerless to treat him, the RUF field medics had simply taped his wounds shut and left him wracked with sweats and shivers.

Throughout the 1990s, children like Lahia armed themselves

with diamond-purchased AK-47s and, under the nose of the UN, helped the rebels sell the gems to terrorists. People had their hands chopped off by RUF units and were sent wandering hopelessly to spread the message of terror. West African 'peacekeepers' were so inept in their defense of Sierra Leone's civilian population that charges of human-rights violations are leveled at them as frequently as they are at the RUF. It is no stretch to say that Sierra Leone disintegrated during the 1990s into a murderous sinkhole of death and torture, all of it fueled by the sale of diamonds to respectable merchants throughout the world.

If nothing else, the story of Sierra Leone's diamond war has proved unequivocally that the world ignores Africa and its problems at its peril. Events far from home often have very tangible impacts, and Sierra Leone has shown the world that there is no longer any such thing as an 'isolated, regional conflict'. Perhaps there never was. ◆

Adapted from an article in
*Amnesty* magazine by Greg Campbell, 2002.

*'Blood diamonds have been both a blessing and a curse for the people of Sierra Leone. In the diamond fields, tens of thousands of impoverished men and children risk their lives in the dream of finding the BIG one.'*

any real controls.' Global Witness recommended that 'all diamonds in trade should carry a Certificate of Origin and be subject to independent scrutiny by internationally recognized diamond experts.'

The report started a scare in the diamond industry and a reaction from the UN. It became clear that the problem was not just in Angola, but also in the Democratic Republic of Congo (DRC), Sierra Leone, and Liberia, which funneled the diamonds illegally to buyers in the West in order to purchase weapons. In each case, diamonds were not only funding the rebels, but also giving them the freedom to behave exactly as they liked.

## Violence in DR Congo

In the DRC, violence had left 2.5 million dead and millions of people displaced or refugees. Hundreds of millions of dollars in diamonds were stolen or smuggled out every year. Liberia does not have any diamonds to speak of, but under the rule of warlord/president Charles Taylor was supporting and funding smuggling from other countries to the West. Taylor is now wanted for war crimes after backing rebels in Sierra Leone.

There, the decade-long civil war had left more than 50,000 dead, half a million refugees and thousands of amputees. Cutting off people's hands was one of the grisly trademarks of the Revolutionary United Front (RUF), the rebel force. The RUF controlled many of the country's diamond mines. A UN report, published in December 2000 estimated that the RUF's diamond trade amounted to at least $25 million and possibly as much as $125 million in diamonds per year in the late 1990s.

As if to prove that such conflicts are indeed global, the complex web of smuggled diamonds was also purported to have funded al-Qaeda, directly or indirectly leading to the attacks of 11 September 2001.

## Diamond deals

An article in *The Washington Post* in November 2001 by journalist Douglas Farah, who was based in Freetown, Sierra Leone, said: 'The terrorist network led by Osama bin Laden has reaped millions of dollars in the past three years from the illicit sale of diamonds mined by rebels in Sierra Leone, according to US and European intelligence officials and two sources with direct knowledge of events.

'Diamond dealers working directly with men named by the FBI as key operatives in bin Laden's al-Qaeda network bought gems from the rebels at below-market prices and sold them for large profits in Europe.' The article resulted in death threats for Farah, who then had to leave the country.

## The Kimberley Process

The UN defines 'conflict diamonds' as those which 'originate from areas controlled by forces or factions opposed to legitimate and internationally recognized governments, and are used to fund military action in opposition to those governments, or in contravention of the decisions of the Security Council'.

As a result of the furor, in 2000 the South African Government called together more than 20 nations in Kimberley. It was the start of negotiations between governments, international organizations and the industry for what became known as the Kimberley Process. Formally launched in 2002, its aim is to control the trade in rough diamonds by establishing minimum acceptable international standards for certification. According to the proposal, participant countries have to ensure that:

**1** Rough diamonds are imported and exported in tamper-resistant containers, accompanied by a Kimberley Process Certificate certifying the country of origin, identification of exporter and importer, carat weight/mass and value.

**2** No shipment of rough diamonds is imported from or exported to a non-participant.

**3** A system of internal controls is established that is designed to eliminate the presence of conflict diamonds from shipments of rough diamonds imported into and exported from its territory.

**4** Appropriate laws or regulations are amended or enacted to implement and enforce the certification scheme and to maintain dissuasive and proportional penalties for transgressions.

**5** Relevant official production, import and export data are collected and maintained.

By April 2004, 43 governments had ratified and adopted the Kimberley Process Certification Scheme, which was fully implemented in August 2003.

However, despite a promising beginning, the Process soon became bogged down. The General Accounting Office, the investigative arm of the US Congress,

---

The jungle is dark but full of diamonds
A diamond is rough and hard to the touch
It's dark there, but full of diamonds

*Arthur Miller*, US playwright.

---

said in a February 2002 report that it was inherently flawed: 'The period after rough diamonds enter the first foreign port until the final point of sale is covered by a system of voluntary industry participation and self-regulated monitoring and enforcement. These and other shortcomings provide significant challenges in creating an effective scheme to deter trade in conflict diamonds.'

The industry is keen to continue to clean up its image. Andrew Bone, chief media officer of De Beers Diamond Trading Company said in an interview: 'No-one in this industry is going to hide behind wringing hands, or a hearts-on-your-sleeve kind of thing... There is a big moral dimension to this, but we're very happy to talk about the enormous commercial loss and gain potential of this as well. And the enormous long-term benefit for West Africa in the industry remains unharmed... Yes, let's get rid of conflict diamonds. We've got more to gain than anyone else on this, apart from the victims. The next big prize is for the industry if we can get rid of this.'

De Beers as usual took the initiative and stopped buying diamonds on the open market. Instead, it sourced them from its own mines and other countries where it has marketing joint ventures with local producers. True to form, it also created a new marketing idea on the back of the conflict diamonds, a branded stone that it said guaranteed the diamond was conflict-free. 'Conflict diamonds were one of the greatest marketing tools ever invented,' said one anonymous South African trader.

But there are still problems. 'De Beers' system is based on the mixing of all supplies into one production for sale. The origin of the diamonds is deliberately obscured for commercial and logistical reasons,' Emma Muller, a journalist specializing in the diamond industry, wrote in South Africa's *Business Day* in March 2002.

There are real difficulties with tracing the paper trail of a diamond. And once cut, it is impossible to tell which mine, or even which country, a stone comes from. Tom Shane, of jewelry retailers Shane Company Inc, one of the largest US importers of polished diamonds, says: 'It's a known fact that if you take a diamond out of the blue and you give it to any expert, they cannot tell where the giddied thing came from. You take a diamond that's been cut and polished and there's no human being on earth who can tell with certainty where that stone came from.'

**The situation today**

In 2005, a group including De Beers and Global Witness (GW) as well as others from the diamond industry, non-governmental organizations and the donor community, set up the Diamond Development Initiative. This recognized that there were still problems, particularly with the one million artisan miners who are outside the Kimberley Process, and sought to deal with this by getting everyone involved to look at solutions. The arrest of former Liberian President Charles Taylor in March 2006 was hailed as a step on the way to international justice; Taylor had used revenues from diamonds in Sierra Leone to prop up his own regime and to support the RUF rebels.

## Jewelers' survey

In 2004, Amnesty International and GW began a global survey of 800 diamond retailers and suppliers in Australia, Belgium, France, Germany, Italy, The Netherlands and Switzerland. Letters were also sent to 85 major jewelry retailers, and Amnesty International activists visited 579 stores in the US and UK. The main findings were presented to the World Diamond Congress in New York:

♦ Despite an industry commitment to educate employees about company diamond regulations, staff in only 42 per cent of stores were aware of their company's policy.

♦ Out of 85 companies that were sent letters requesting written information about their policies, 48 (56 per cent) failed to respond including major diamond jewelry retailers such as Osprey, Theo Fennell and Debenhams in the UK, and Costco Whole Sale Corporation, TK Maxx and Kmart in the US.

♦ 32 out of the 37 companies that responded (86 per cent) are implementing the system of warranties and have a policy to prevent dealing in conflict diamonds. However 30 of the companies responding (81 per cent) did not provide adequate details on how the system of warranties is being implemented and audited.

'The continued lack of systematic monitoring throughout the diamond industry suggests that the industry is not taking the issue seriously enough,' said Alessandra Masci of Amnesty International.

In 2005, Global Witness released a report 'Making it Work: why the Kimberley Process must do more to stop conflict diamonds'. GW's Susie Sanders stated: 'The Kimberley Process has taken real steps to stop the trade in conflict diamonds, but the problem has not been solved. Governments must audit all sectors of the diamond trade and take credible action against members of the diamond industry that are known to trade in conflict diamonds. In addition, the UN Security Council should place sanctions on diamonds from Côte d'Ivoire (see below).'

The report shows how:

♦ Some members of the diamond industry continue to evade the Kimberley Process controls, while others turn a blind eye. Diamonds from Cote d'Ivoire are being mined in rebel-held areas and are then smuggled through neighboring countries to international markets.

♦ Despite being subject to UN sanctions, Liberian

---

## WANT TO BUY A CONFLICT-FREE DIAMOND?

Unfortunately, people who buy diamonds don't really want to think about where they come from. 'The fact of the matter is that to the consumer it's a very low interest issue,' said Tom Shane of US jewelers Shane Company Inc. 'Even with all the articles that have been written, we don't hear it in our stores being raised as an issue'.

Global Witness recommends asking four questions if you are buying a diamond:

♦ How can I be sure that none of your jewelry contains conflict diamonds?

♦ Do I know where the diamonds you sell come from?

♦ Can I see a copy of your company's policy on conflict diamonds?

♦ Can you show me a written guarantee from your diamond suppliers stating that your diamonds are conflict-free? ♦

---

## FOR THE TIMES,
## THEY AREN'T A-CHANGIN'

Bob Dylan's song 'A Hard Rain's A-Gonna Fall' (extract below) from 1963 might have written for the 21st century.

*'Oh, what did you see, my blue-eyed son?*
*Oh, what did you see, my darling young one?*
*I saw a newborn baby with wild wolves all around it*
*I saw a highway of diamonds with nobody on it,*
*I saw a black branch with blood that kept drippin',*
*I saw a room full of men with their hammers a-bleedin',*
*I saw a white ladder all covered with water,*
*I saw ten thousand talkers whose tongues were all broken,*
*I saw guns and sharp swords in the hands of young children,*
*And it's a hard, and it's a hard, it's a hard, it's a hard,*
*And it's a hard rain's a-gonna fall.'*

diamonds are being smuggled into neighboring countries and certified by the Kimberley Process.

◆ Weak regulation of diamond cutting and polishing factories leaves centers vulnerable to the trade in conflict diamonds.

In December 2005 the UN Security Council broadened the arms embargo on Côte d'Ivoire to include a ban on diamond exports. In 2000 a study for the World Diamond Council said that: ' Based upon current knowledge, we do not know of any scientific way to determine the country of origin of rough or polished gem diamonds, nor do we foresee practical ways being developed in the near future.' The problem of conflict diamonds hasn't gone away. And it is unlikely to do so in a hurry.

# 5

# From ring to bling

'I prefer a man who lives
And gives expensive jewels.'

— FROM 'DIAMONDS ARE A GIRL'S BEST FRIEND'
BY LEO ROBIN AND JULE STYNE.

**Diamonds are a symbol of love, wealth and fame. So** what is it that makes us think they are so special? They sparkle, but so does cubic zirconium. They are rare, but not as rare as rubies. They are billions of years old, but so are fossils. These qualities can account for the historical belief in their magical properties and the fact that people from queens of the realm to kings of hip-hop have used them for adornment – but not for why it is only a diamond that will do as a token of a person's love for another, or why someone – usually a man – is prepared to spend two months' salary on a tiny gem to prove that love.

## ADVERTISING SHINE

**Harry Oppenheimer, director of De Beers for 60 years, told the story of how the company got involved in advertising, in one of the last interviews he gave before his death in 2000.**

It's a curious thing, but when I was first in business, and the idea of advertising diamonds was first mooted, there was a belief among a great many more senior directors that if you advertise diamonds you somehow cheapen them, and that would have an adverse effect on our sales.

Then there was a move, particularly by Frank Myer who was the deputy chairman of De Beers at the time, to advertise diamonds, but in a very specialized way. He had the idea that we should approach leading dress designers of the 1930s, especially Chanel, who were all using elaborate fake jewelry to go with their great dresses. In the event, Frank thought that Madame Chanel should be persuaded to design real diamond jewelry, and she was willing to do this, for a certain price. I don't think she was very good at designing jewelry. Anyhow she did so; but

The answer, however, is simple. Advertising. It began in earnest back in 1938. Diamond engagement rings were not yet widely used in Europe and De Beers was worried about the effect that the impending war might have on European sales. While most of De Beer's sales went to America, the diamonds sold there were of an inferior of course it had no effect whatsoever.

After this I persuaded my father to let me go over to America to see what I could find out about the possibility of advertising diamonds. It was obvious that if it were to be done at all it would have to be there, because the US was then, even more than now, the main market for diamonds. I saw various advertising people and finally I hit upon NW Ayer, which was one of the more reputable firms in New York. NW Ayer said to me that while they thought diamonds had great potential, the first thing one needed to do was to make an enquiry into why people buy diamonds in the first place, which was a fairly novel approach back then. They conducted a survey and came to the conclusion that the high fashion side of selling diamonds was just a bit of icing on the cake and not important at all, and that the real reason people buy diamonds is because they are a symbol of love. The whole advertising campaign subsequently designed by NW Ayer was based on this premise and it has continued along the same lines ever since. ◆

quality to those sold in Europe. A new strategy was needed: De Beers' director Harry Oppenheimer found it on a visit to New York (see box).

In a survey, the De Beers' advertising agency NW Ayer found that people bought diamonds as a symbol of love. The survey also found that since 1919, the total amount of diamonds sold in America, measured in carats, had declined by 50 per cent. An Ayer memo noted that this was 'the result of the economy, changes in social attitudes and the promotion of competitive luxuries.'

Ten years later, a woman copywriter in NW Ayer came up with the slogan 'A diamond is forever'. She may not have known it, but she was building on Cecil Rhodes, who had said that his empire would continue to grow as long as 'men and women continue to fall in love'. NW Ayer wanted to make absolutely sure that love and diamonds went together. They embarked on an all-out marketing plan that included product placement in films and on television, radio programs publicizing diamond trends, and portraits of celebrities wearing diamond engagement rings. One campaign in the top American magazines such as *Fortune, The New Yorker, Time* and *Vogue* featured the paintings of famous artists like Picasso, Derain, Dali and Dufy together with diamonds.

By 1941 sales of diamonds in the US were up 55 per cent. The same successes were repeated further afield. In 1959, De Beers hired J Walter Thompson to promote diamonds in Japan. At that time the Japanese Government did not allow the import of diamonds, nor did the tradition of gifts exchanged at the time a marriage was arranged include diamond rings. It took 14 years, but by 1981, 60 per cent of married women wore a diamond ring and Japanese men were spending more than their American counterparts – three to four months' salary – to prove their devotion.

The power of the 'diamond is forever' concept continues well into the 21st century. Eighty per cent of gemstone diamonds are bought as engagement rings or for wedding anniversaries. New ideas are constantly being thought

---

## A DIAMOND IS...

♦ Horse equipment: 'Double Diamond Halter Company offers the finest handmade rope halters. Built by cowboys, tested by broncs.'

♦ Warm English beer: Double Diamond Original Burton Ale has been brewed since 1876. It takes its name from the twin diamonds symbol which used to be chalked on each wooden cask to denote the finest of ales. 'A Double Diamond works wonders' was a slogan.

♦ A computer game: Diamond Mine Game – 'Catch some gem-matching fun with this supercharged Windows version of the hit online puzzle game, featuring hi-res graphics, awesome sound effects, and a brand new killer soundtrack, along with the classic gameplay Bejeweled Game fans know and love, a new Diamond Mine Game for you!' ♦

---

up by diamond companies, for example in China, where the market continues to grow, a diamond wedding ring is being successfully promoted to over half of married couples in the top 25 cities.

When small diamonds from the Soviet Union started to flood the market in the 1960s, De Beers instructed NW Ayer to 'illustrate gems as small as one-tenth of a carat and give them the same emotional importance as larger stones.' Eternity rings, with up to 25 smaller diamonds, were promoted for wedding anniversaries. The average size of diamonds sold fell from one carat in 1939 to .28 of a carat in 1976, which coincided almost exactly with the average size of Soviet diamonds. This nearly caused a problem, as women turned away from larger rings, seeing them as 'ostentatious', but a new advertising campaign promoted the larger gems as well in order to get around this hurdle.

By 1979, the value of De Beers' sales in the US had increased from $23 million in 1939 to $2.1 billion.

## The element of surprise

In the 1970s NW Ayer commissioned an opinion poll which revealed that when men give a diamond to a woman, it is often as a surprise. 'Approximately half of all diamond jewelry that the men have given and the women have received was given with zero participation or knowledge on the part of the woman recipient... Women are in unanimous agreement that they want to be surprised with gifts... They want, of course, to be surprised for the thrill of it. However, a deeper, more important reason lies behind this desire... "freedom from guilt". Some of the women pointed out that if their husbands enlisted their help in purchasing a gift (like diamond jewelry), their practical nature would come to the fore and they would be compelled to object to the purchase.'

The study went on to point out that the man giving the diamond plays a very traditional active role, while the woman is the passive recipient. The diamond is a symbol

---

**TROPHY WIVES**

'It's a big deal for working people to buy a diamond,' he told his sons, 'no matter how small. The wife can wear it for the beauty and she can wear it for the status. And when she does, this guy is not just a plumber – he's a man with a wife with a diamond. His wife owns something that is imperishable. Because beyond the beauty and the status and the value, the diamond is imperishable. A piece of the earth that is imperishable, and a mere mortal is wearing it on her hand!' ◆

Philip Roth, *Everyman* (Jonathan Cape 2006) p 57.

not only of seduction, but of status and wealth.

More recently, De Beers' Trilogy campaign, promoted a ring with three diamonds symbolizing 'Past, Present and Future'. In the US sales of the Trilogy grew by 35 per cent in 2004 and retail sales were worth $3 billion. In Japan, the campaign links diamonds with personal contentment and Trilogy rings now account for 13 per cent of the Japanese market.

In January 1999 the magazine *American Age* proclaimed 'A Diamond is Forever' to be the most recognized and effective slogan of the 20th century, recognized by 90 per cent of Americans.

### Diamonds and celebrities

In the past, it was kings and queens who saw diamonds as a royal prerogative. They were the celebrities of their day, but after the De Beers campaign it was increasingly movie stars and singers who give diamonds their glitter. Most are women. It has become *de rigeur* to wear diamonds at the Oscars: wearers of the gems include Madonna, Gwyneth Paltrow, Cate Blanchett, Nicole Kidman, Julia Roberts and Sharon Stone. Some, like Liz Taylor (see box below), wear their own jewels, but many simply rent them for the occasion, often from US diamond giant Harry Winston

## JOHN LENNON, AND LUCY

When the Beatles' album *Sergeant Pepper's Lonely Hearts Club Band* was released in 1967, its centerpiece track was the song that featured John Lennon singing drug-inspired lyrics. It wasn't long, however, before listeners discovered the 'hidden' pun in the song's title, 'Lucy in the Sky with Diamonds': the initial letters of certain words spelled out 'LSD'.

John Lennon, while never denying that the song itself was inspired by the acid trips he had taken, quickly explained that the title, in fact, had been mere coincidence. It was taken from the title John's 4-year-old son Julian had given to a drawing he made at school. Impressed with his son's handiwork, John asked what the drawing was called. 'It's Lucy in the Sky with Diamonds, Daddy,' Julian replied.

Lennon says he had no idea that the title formed the abbreviation LSD until it was pointed out to him by someone else after the album's release. In a 1970 interview with *Rolling Stone* magazine he said of the song's title: 'I swear to God, or swear to Mao, or to anybody you like, I had no idea it spelled LSD...' ◆

Inc., who have been loaning jewels to the stars since 1943. In 2002, Halle Berry wore a $3 million orange diamond ring from Harry Winston.

'We've never lost anything,' says James Kersey from Harry Winston. However, 'one year Madonna gave us quite a scare. She was singing the nominated song from the film *Dick Tracy* and wearing an incredible amount of jewelry... At the end of the number, she took one of the earrings and threw it into the audience.' The jewelers had not been told that she had replaced them with costume jewelry just before going on stage.

Sometimes the gems are so valuable that they need to be guarded: *Mulholland Drive* actress Laura Harring had three bodyguards when she wore diamond-studded shoes worth a million dollars and $27 million worth around her neck.

But like everything in Hollywood, the jewels are something of a fairytale. They say a diamond is forever, but these gems were all marked return to sender. Unless of course you're Sharon Stone. In 1994, the *Basic Instinct* star donned a $500,000 Harry Winston necklace which she assumed – wrongly – was a gift. She eventually gave up the jewels, but only after filing a misrepresentation suit against the venerable firm.

No wonder the sparklers make these women feel like a million dollars – and their fans believe they are worth the same amount.

Diamonds are no longer just something worn by famous women. Men have also started wearing jewelry. For his

# BIG GIRLS NEED BIG DIAMONDS

Actor Richard Burton was famous not just in his own right and for being Elizabeth Taylor's fifth husband, but for buying her fabulous diamonds. 'I would have liked to buy her the Taj Mahal,' he remarked, 'but it would cost too much to transport. '

He bought her the 33.19-carat emerald-cut Krupp diamond in 1968. Next came the magnificent pearl known as La Peregrina. For her 40th birthday he gave her a heart-shaped diamond set with rubies in a pendant. But the most famous gift was a 69.42 carat jewel that came to be known as the Taylor-Burton diamond. It was cut from a rough stone weighing 240.80 carats found in South Africa's Premier Mine in 1966 and subsequently bought by Harry Winston Inc. 'Big girls need big diamonds,' Liz Taylor is reputed to have said.

Burton actually lost the auction for the diamond in 1969. The winner, Robert Kenmore, who had bought it for $1,050,000, sold it on to Burton on the understanding that it would be displayed at Cartier's in New York. There it was visited by 6,000 people a day. Elizabeth Taylor wore it in public for the first time at Princess Grace of Monaco's 40th birthday party. It was flown from New York to Nice in the company of two armed guards. In 1978, after Taylor's divorce from Burton, she said that she was selling the diamond and would use some of the proceeds to build a hospital in Botswana. ◆

26th birthday, Victoria Beckham gave her footballer husband a £5,000-pair of diamond cross earrings. 'David Beckham wearing diamonds has really changed the attitude towards men's jewelry', says a spokesperson for Cartier. 'It's cool for a man to wear diamonds. Being flashy is no longer a problem. The message is: if you've got it, flaunt it'. What David Beckham wears today, the man in the street will want to wear tomorrow. And not just men – kids too. In 2005 the Beckhams splashed out £25,000 ($45,000) on a pair of diamond earrings for their son Brooklyn's sixth birthday. A source close to the couple said: 'Brooklyn adores his father and always wants everything his dad has got. David and Victoria wanted to give him a real special treat for his birthday.'

## Movie diamonds

The diamond industry knew from early on that having a celebrity promote the gems would be the best kind of publicity. De Beers used its influence to modify film scripts and ensure that diamonds were featured prominently. 'Product placement' of diamonds in movies began as early as 1941, with the movie *Skylark*, where the female character shops for diamonds. The 1950s hit *Gentlemen Prefer Blondes* with Marilyn Monroe and Jane Russell

# FALL FROM GRACELAND

In South Africa in the late 1950s, Joseph Shabalala was singing and playing guitar when he was asked by a group to join them in performing music called *isicathamiya*, 'tip-toe guys'.

This music has a long history. In the 19th century, black South Africans were forced to work in the diamond mines. The workers would perform song and dance on Saturday nights, for their only free day was Sunday.

The dancing was so vigorous that sometimes the hut floors would be broken. Complaints by neighbors led to a new quieter dance, *cothoza mfana*, known as 'tip-toe harmony'. This soon spread to the townships where it gained many fans and became known as 'township jive'; still a part of South African culture.

In the 1960s Shabalala formed Ladysmith Black Mambazo. Over the next 15 years the band recorded 25 albums; huge in South Africa but barely known outside the continent, until the *vulindella* ('he who opened the gate') – Paul Simon – arrived. He had heard a bootleg tape of South African music, including Ladysmith. Their recording sessions yielded songs for the hit album, *Graceland* in 1986 – including 'Diamonds on the Soles of her Shoes'.

Global acclaim allowed Ladysmith to perform internationally but they incurred the wrath of the anti-apartheid movement for breaking the cultural boycott. ◆

featured the song 'Diamonds are a Girl's Best Friend'.

Janet Wasko in her book *How Hollywood Works* analyses the product placements in the James Bond film *Die Another Day*, which also happens to focus on the diamond trade. It features over 20 branded products that were not included in the film by accident. Bond drives an Aston Martin, the bad guy (Zao) drives a Jaguar, and the heroine (Jinx) is assigned a Thunderbird. Meanwhile, Range Rovers are used extensively as utility vehicles. Bond drinks Finlandia vodka, sips Bollinger champagne, and shaves with the latest Norelco electric shaver... All of these products were deliberately "placed" in the film. No wonder *Time* magazine suggested that the film might have been called, 'Buy Another Day.'

In 2003, the film *Catwoman* featured Halle Berry wearing a diamond ring on her right hand (not to mention her diamond claws!). In the same year, De Beers launched its campaign 'Women of the World Raise Your Right Hand'. It was targeted at the affluent, fashion-savvy, independent woman who knew what she wanted and was prepared to buy herself a ring. 'The age of marriage is now later than ever before. Women won't wait for a man to get their first diamond', says Susan Farmer of De Beers' Diamond Trading Company. In Britain, women buying their own diamonds now account for 12 per cent of the UK diamond retail sales, against 2 per cent 10 years ago.

## Bling-bling

Today, diamonds are the 'bling'; the 'ice' of the hip-hop scene. 'Details, baby. It's all about the details,' muses "bling-bling" king P Diddy. 'Look at the... ring, the watch. Look at my canary-yellow diamond. Impeccable. Admit it, I am impeccable.' Hip-hop glorifies the lives of the rich and famous and 'bling' or jewelry has been an important part of this. In the 1980s it was gold chains, in the 21st century it is diamonds and platinum. Getting and displaying the 'ice' has been an important part of showing that you have made it. Thousands of websites sprang up offering fake 'bling' to those who cannot afford the real thing.

But recently a number of artists have made songs condemning the trade in blood diamonds (see chapter 4). In 2001 Ms Dynamite wrote the song: 'It Takes More':

*Now who gives a damn*
*about the ice on your hands?*
*If it's not too complex*
*Tell me how many Africans died*
*for the baguettes on your Rolex?*
*So what you pushing a nice car*

*don't you know there's no such thing as superstar*
*we leave this world alone*
*so who gives a fuck about the things you own?*
She was followed by Kanye West, whose song 'Diamonds
from Sierra Leone' had the same message, although he
admitted that it will not stop him wearing the ice: 'That's
what Kanye West is all about, it's the conflict. It's the,
I wanna wear diamonds but I know about this. It's like
damn how do I go about this. Like... I know I shouldn't
have sex before marriage but I'm horny as hell.'

*Good morning, this ain't Vietnam still/*
*People lose hands, legs, arms, for real/*
*Little was known on Sierra Leone/*
*And how it connects to the diamonds we own*

*See, a part of me sayin', "Keep shinin"/*
*How? When I know what's a blood diamond/*
*Though it's thousands of miles away/*
*Sierra Leone connect to what we go through today/*
*Over here it's a drug trade, we die from drugs/*
*Over there they die from what we buy from drugs/*
'Diamonds from Sierra Leone' *by Kanye West*
www.rwdmag.com/artist

# 6

# Are diamonds forever?

'I never hated a man enough to give him diamonds back.'

— 8-TIMES WED ACTRESS
ZSA ZSA GABOR.

**It is very unlikely that the world will run out of** diamonds in the near future; as we have seen in Australia, Russia and Canada in recent years, new sources are constantly being discovered.

But the sale of diamonds as gems depends entirely on people choosing them over other stones. Before NW Ayer's famous slogan 'A diamond is forever' persuaded us that diamonds were the only choice as engagement rings, opals, rubies, sapphires and turquoise were seen as the exotic and expensive gems to be given as a token of love. Big companies like De Beers continue to spend in order to persuade us to buy diamonds. Around 100 million women today wear the glittering prizes.

However, you could say we are being conned. For diamonds are two a penny – they are so ubiquitous. Yet they are still sold to the public as if they are a rarity, and that buying one for someone is an act of singular devotion and demonstration of wealth.

In addition, while the gems may sparkle as a token of love, they are not necessarily such a good investment. Unless you lose them, or they are stolen, they do last forever, and so every gem that has been bought is still in existence today. In a 1982 article entitled 'Have You Ever Tried to Sell a Diamond?' Edward Jay Epstein cites a survey in 1970 for *Which?* magazine to test how much a diamond increased in value over 10 years. It bought two gem-quality diamonds, weighing approximately one-half carat apiece, from one of London's most reputable diamond dealers, for £400 (then worth about $1,000). For nearly 9 years, it kept these 2 diamonds sealed in an envelope in its vault.

**Poor investment**

During this same period, Britain experienced inflation that ran as high as 25 per cent a year. For the diamonds to have kept pace with inflation, they would have had to increase in value at least 300 per cent... But when the magazine's editor, Dave Watts, tried to sell the diamonds in 1978, he found that neither jewelry stores nor wholesale dealers in London's Hatton Garden district would pay anywhere near that price for the diamonds. Most of the stores refused to pay any cash for them; the highest bid Watts received was £500, which amounted to a profit of only £100 in over 8 years, or less than 3 per cent at a compound rate of interest. If the bid were calculated in 1970 pounds, it would amount to only £167. Dave Watts summed up the magazine's experiment by saying, 'As an 8-year investment the diamonds that we bought have proved to be very poor.' The problem was that the buyer, not the seller, determined the price. A similar experiment was conducted in 1976, by the Dutch Consumer Association, which bought a one-carat diamond in Amsterdam, kept it for eight months, and then offered it for sale to Amsterdam's 20 main dealers. Nineteen refused to buy it, and the twentieth only offered a fraction of the purchase price.

Those who try to sell their diamonds may find themselves cheated. There are lots of people making money out of buying and selling diamonds. And not all of it is legal. Diamondhelpers.com lists 20 common diamond scams, which include things like switching the diamond, listing the total carat weight of the diamond rather than that of the central stone, exaggerating the carat weight or rounding it off, laser-drilling out flaws, faking certificates. It notes: 'minor scams are very common and are found in almost all of the major jewelry chain stores to some degree,' and advises against buying from the diamond district in New York.

## A diamond crash?

It is estimated that at least 500 million carats' worth of diamonds are stored under beds and in bank vaults. If a significant portion of those women decided to sell their diamonds, the market would collapse.

One dealer painted a gloomy picture of what might happen: 'Investment diamonds are bought for $30,000 a carat, not because any woman wants to wear them on her finger but because the investor believes they will be worth $50,000 a carat. He may borrow heavily to leverage his investment. When the price begins to decline, everyone will try to sell their diamonds at once. In the end, of course, there will be no buyers for diamonds at $30,000 a carat or even $15,000. At this point, there will be a stampede to sell investment diamonds, and the newspapers will begin writing stories about the great diamond crash. Investment diamonds constitute, of course, only a small fraction of the diamonds held by the public, but when women begin reading about a diamond crash, they will take their diamonds to retail jewelers to be appraised and find out that they are worth less than they paid for them. At that point, people will realize that diamonds are not forever, and jewelers will be flooded with customers trying to sell, not buy, diamonds. That will be the end of the diamond business.' But this was back in 1982, and it has not happened yet.

## The modern alchemists

When Sir John Mandeville said in 1366 that he could grow diamonds, he was not being so far-fetched after all. In 1796, diamonds were discovered to be carbon, and many people tried to make them. But it was only in the 1950s that Swedish and American researchers found the answer. Graphite, also made of carbon, could be made into diamond by seeding small diamonds, applying huge pressures, heat of over 1,400°C, and molten iron. It takes a few days to grow diamonds a few millimeters across, and only tens of minutes to grow micro diamonds. But to date, the diamonds produced in this way have been small, a maximum of 2 carats in the 1970s, and suitable only for industrial use. It was only in 2005 that the technology was developed to produce larger gems that could be used for other purposes. It is called chemical vapor deposition, or CVD.

CVD has ramifications not only for the jewelry industry, but also in a range of technologies, including a possible and much faster replacement for the microchip. Kevin Maney of *USA Today* says: 'In technology, the diamond is a dream material. It can make computers run at speeds that would melt the innards of today's computers. Manufactured diamonds could help make lasers of extreme power. The material could allow a cell phone to fit into a watch and iPods to store 10,000 movies, not just 10,000 songs. Diamonds could mean frictionless medical replacement joints. Or coatings – perhaps for cars – that never scratch or wear out... The ability to manufacture diamonds could change business, products and daily life as much as the arrival of the steel age in the 1850s or the invention of the transistor in the 1940s.'

Diamonds may be about to start another revolution. And it could be even more dramatic than it was when they were discovered in South Africa in 1870 and changed the face of a continent.

The ancient gem still has a few more surprises up its sleeve. But perhaps we can do without diamonds – and other precious gems – altogether? GreenKarat is an organization advocating an 'end to destructive gold and diamond mining.' They suggest that the real power to bring change rests with us, the consumers: 'While activist organizations play a critically important role in educating and motivating consumers, we believe that widespread and permanent change will ultimately occur through the voice of consumer buying decisions. Our mission is to provide an ecologically and socially responsible jewelry alternative to those who seek change.' They believe 'it is time to phase out diamond mining altogether.'

All that glitters is not good.

# RESOURCES

**WEBSITES**
**Amnesty** www.amnestyusa.org/diamonds/index.do
Details on conflict diamonds.
**American Natural History Museum**
www.amnh.org/exhibitions/diamonds/
Packed with facts on all aspects of diamonds including history and mining.
**Canadian Government** www.iti.gov.nt.ca/diamond/industry.htm
Lots of information on diamonds around the world.
**De Beers** www.debeersgroup.com/debeersweb
The De Beers site.
**Global Witness** www.globalwitness.org/campaigns/diamonds/
The Global Witness diamond campaign.
**How stuff works** http://people.howstuffworks.com/diamond7.htm Quirky
information.
**www.edwardjayepstein.com/diamond.htm**
Good background; exposes myth of scarcity and 'forever'-ness.
**www.ex.ac.uk/~RDavies/arian/scandals/diamonds.html**
Diamond scandals and other information.
**United Nations** www.un.org/peace/africa/Diamond.html
Analysis of blood diamonds.
**Green Karat – 'Jewelry without Cruelty'** calls for diamond mining
to be banned. www.greenkarat.com/about/philosophy.asp

# BOOKS

**FICTION**
**Diamonds are Forever** Ian Fleming (Penguin, latest edition 2002)
**Heart of the Matter** Graham Greene (Penguin, 1948)
**Wilderness of Mirrors** Linda Davies (Orion, 1996)

**NON-FICTION**
**Blood Diamonds** Greg Campbell (Westview Press, 2004)
**The Last Empire: De Beers, Diamonds and the World** Stefan Kanfer
(Coronet, 1993)
**Glitter and Greed: the secret world of the diamond cartel** Janine Roberts
(The Disinformation Company, 2003)